KT-437-413

Journey's End

1   3

Dartford Library
Tel: 01322 221153
Fax: 01322 278271
dartfordlibrary@kent.gov.uk

10. MAY 04

23/03/07

WITHDRAWN

393   Books should be returned or renewed by the
last date stamped above

GANERI, A.

Journey's End

Awarded for excellence
to Arts & Libraries

Kent
County
Council

Evans

EVANS BROTHERS LIMITED

C151628153   DAR

INTRODUCTION

KENT
ARTS & LIBRARIES
C151628153
393

In each of the world's six major religions, the most important times in a person's life are marked by special ceremonies. These are a bit like signposts on the journey through life, guiding a person from one stage of their life to the next. They also give people the chance to share their beliefs and their joys or sorrows, whether in celebrating a baby's birth, the change from child to adult, a wedding, or marking and remembering a person's death. For each occasion, there are prayers to be said, presents to give and receive, festive food to eat and stories to tell. Customs and ceremonies vary in different parts of the world. This book looks at just some of them.

JOURNEY'S END

This book examines how people from the Hindu, Buddhist, Sikh, Jewish, Christian and Muslim faiths mark a person's death. Each faith has its own funeral customs and rituals which help its followers to cope with the death of a loved one. Each faith also has its own beliefs about what becomes of us after we die.

In this book dates are written with BCE and CE, instead of BC and AD which are based on the Christian calendar. BCE means 'Before the Common Era' and it replaces BC (Before Christ). CE means 'in the Common Era' and it replaces AD (Anno Domini 'in the year of our Lord').

 This is the Hindu sacred symbol 'Om'. It expresses all the secrets of the universe.

 This wheel is a Buddhist symbol. Its eight spokes stand for eight points of the Buddha's teaching.

 This Sikh symbol is called the 'Ik onkar'. It means: 'There is only one God'.

 The Star of David is a Jewish symbol. It appears on the flag of Israel.

 The cross is a Christian symbol. It reminds Christians of how Jesus died on a cross.

 The star and crescent moon are symbols of Islam.

CONTENTS

MANY LIVES

The rites and rituals performed when a Hindu dies are the last of 16 special ceremonies, called samskaras. These begin at birth and mark the important times in a Hindu's life. For Hindus, death is not the end of everything. They believe that a person lives many lives and dies many deaths before being united with Brahman, the great soul or spirit who created the universe.

Sacred words

These are two passages from the Hindu sacred books that are read at funerals:

'This soul within my heart is smaller than a grain of rice, or a mustard seed, or a kernel of millet.
This soul within my heart is greater than the earth, the air, the sky
And all the worlds.
This is my soul within my heart.
This is the All.
And when I die, I shall merge into it.'

'When a person's clothes wear out, he leaves them behind
and puts on new and different ones.
And so the soul leaves a worn-out body and puts on a new and different one.'

Being reborn

Hindus believe that when a person dies, his or her soul lives on and is reborn in another body, human or animal. This is called reincarnation. You are reborn again and again unless you break free of the cycle of reincarnation and gain moksha, or salvation. Moksha is when your soul is united with Brahman. Your next life depends on how you live your present life. If you behave well, you will be reborn closer to moksha. Bad behaviour means moving further away from moksha. This process is called karma. Karma is the belief that all actions have their effects, good and bad.

A Hindu funeral

When a Hindu dies, the body is washed and dressed in new clothes. Sweet-smelling sandalwood paste is rubbed on the dead

As the mourners carry the body to the cremation ground, they chant the name of the god, Rama.

person's forehead. The family priest helps with all the rituals. In India, the body is then covered with a white or orange cloth and placed on a bamboo stretcher. It is carried to the cremation ground outside the village or town. Here it is placed on a large platform of logs and sandalwood, called a funeral pyre. The eldest son, or a close male relative, lights the fire while the priest chants verses from the Hindu sacred books. These remind the mourners that even though the physical body dies, the soul lives on. Melted butter, or ghee, is poured on the fire to make it burn and as an offering to the gods. An important moment is when the person's skull cracks and releases his or her soul for rebirth. Burning the body is the way of offering it to Agni, god of fire.

The body is burned on a funeral pyre of logs and sweet-smelling sandalwood.

A time of mourning

After the funeral, the family go home and observe ten or 12 days of mourning. The men do not shave and no sweet dishes are prepared in the house. The family say prayers and make offerings of rice balls and milk, called pinda, at their family shrine. This is to make sure the person's soul has a safe journey. A final ceremony takes place on the tenth or 12th day. Once this is over, Hindus believe that the person's soul has found a new body.

White for mourning

In the Hindu religion, white is the colour of mourning. A Hindu widow wears a plain white sari, with very little jewellery. She also removes the red mark she has worn on her forehead since she was married.

A Hindu widow in a white sari

The cremation grounds along the River Ganges in Varanasi. The city is considered a very holy place to die. A dead person's ashes are scattered in the sacred waters of the Ganges.

The sacred river

In India, three days after the funeral, the family returns to the cremation ground to collect the ashes. They scatter the ashes in the River Ganges. Hindus believe that the water of the Ganges washes away sins and brings them closer to moksha. The Ganges is especially holy at the sacred city of Varanasi. Many Hindus try to spend their last days in Varanasi so they can be cremated on the river bank. By dying in such a holy place, they hope to be saved from many rebirths.

Outside India

Hindus living outside India have to adapt the traditional funeral service and hold it in a local crematorium. Many families make a special journey to India to scatter the ashes in the River Ganges.

The river of heaven

This is the story of how the River Ganges fell to Earth from its source in heaven.

There was once a very holy king, called Bhagiratha, who worshipped the god Shiva. The king begged Shiva to let the Ganges fall to Earth to bring his dead ancestors back to life. Shiva agreed but he knew the Earth would shatter under the water's great weight. So he caught the river in his long, tangled hair and let it trickle gently down to the Himalayas. The king led the water from the mountains, right across India to the sea and down into the land of the dead. There its sacred waters touched the ashes of his ancestors and brought them back to life.

A NEW JOURNEY

Buddhists believe in reincarnation. When people die, they are reborn, depending on their karma (see page 6). Breaking free of the cycle of reincarnation is called nirvana. This is a state of perfect peace and happiness, reached by people who have realised the true meaning of life and gained enlightenment.

Five skandhas

Buddhists believe that everyone is made up of five parts – their body, feelings, awareness, understanding and will. The way these parts are put together makes everyone different and changes each time a person is reborn.

A Buddhist funeral

The Buddha taught that everything changes and nothing lasts for ever. Dying is part of the natural process of change. Buddhists try to remember his words when someone dies and not feel too sad. Monks attend the funeral to chant prayers and verses from the sacred texts. Everyone repeats their commitment to the Three Jewels of

When a Buddhist dies, the body is usually cremated. At some funerals, the body is carried to the cremation ground on a beautifully decorated platform like this one in Indonesia.

Buddhism. These are the Buddha, the dharma (his teaching) and the sangha (the Buddhist community). They also recite the Five Precepts, or Promises. They promise not to harm living things, not to steal, have affairs, tell lies or take drugs or alcohol. These are the most important Buddhist beliefs. The dead person is usually cremated.

Sacred stupas

When the Buddha died, his ashes were divided up and placed inside eight dome-shaped shrines, called stupas. These were built in places important to him. Today, there are stupas all over the Buddhist world. Some hold the ashes of important monks. Others contain sacred texts.

The Swayambunath Stupa in Kathmandu, Nepal

The Buddha passes away

After many years of travelling around India and teaching his message, the Buddha reached the little town of Kushinagara. He was 80 years old. A local blacksmith invited him to his house for a meal. Some time later, the Buddha fell ill. With his trusty disciple, Ananda, he made his way to a grove of shady trees. There he lay down on his right-hand side. He told Ananda not to be sad and reminded him that everything has to end. Then he passed away and entered nirvana. That night, an earthquake shook the Earth, just as when the Buddha was born.

A RESTING SOUL

Sikhs think of death as a long sleep during which a person's soul rests for a while before beginning a new life. Although they are sad when a loved one dies, they believe that this is God's will and that God is always watching over them.

Beliefs about death

Sikhs gathering for a funeral. Although this is a sad time, the mourners sing hymns to remind them that death is God's will.

Sikhs believe that a person's soul comes from God and will, when they die, return to live with God. This depends on karma (see page 6) but also on the grace of God. If a person worships God with all their heart and follows the teachings of the gurus, then God will set them free from the cycle of death and rebirth, and their soul will be with

God. This is called mukti, or salvation. To reach mukti, a Sikh must be gurmukh, or 'filled with God'.

Hymns and duties

When a Sikh dies, people sing hymns and read from the *Guru Granth Sahib*, the holy book of the Sikhs, to comfort the person's family. Then the body is washed with a mixture of water and yoghurt, and dressed in a new set of clothes. These clothes include the Five Ks which are important symbols of

Before the coffin is taken to the gurdwara, people file past it to pay their last respects to the person who has died. Some say a few words to express their sorrow.

the Sikh faith. They are kesh (uncut hair), kanga (a comb), kara (an iron bracelet), kirpan (a sword) and kaccha (shorts). Men often wear a turban. Then the body is placed in a coffin and covered with a plain cloth or shawl.

The funeral service

The funeral procession begins with prayers. Then, in India, the coffin is carried to the funeral pyre. In Western countries, the coffin is taken to the local crematorium, often in an undertaker's hearse. A prayer is said for the person's soul, then the pyre is lit by the eldest son, or a close male relation. More prayers are said as the fire burns.

The evening prayer

The most important prayer at the funeral is the Sohila, or evening prayer. Sikhs also use this prayer at the end of each day. It reminds them to serve God and not to be afraid of dying. This is part of the prayer:

'Know the real reason why you are here. Collect up your treasure under the true Guru's guidance. Make your mind God's home. If God is with you always, you will not be reborn.'

At the gurdwara

After the funeral, the mourners go to the gurdwara where they listen to readings from the *Guru Granth Sahib*. The service ends with the Ardas prayer, said at the end of all Sikh services. It reminds the mourners to think about God and the ten Gurus. It also asks God to look after all people. Then everyone shares karah parshad (a sweet made of flour, sugar and water). This shows that everyone is equal, a very important Sikh belief.

In the gurdwara, the coffin is placed facing the Guru Granth Sahib, *the Sikhs' holy book. More people come to pay their last respects.*

After the funeral

The dead person's ashes are scattered in a river or in the sea. Sikhs do not believe in putting up gravestones in the person's memory. They prefer to remember people for their good deeds. Over the next 14 days, friends and relations visit the family to offer their sympathy. Every year a ceremony is held to remember the person who died.

Sharing karah parshad at the end of a funeral service. This reminds people that life must go on even though a loved one has died.

The death of Guru Nanak

Guru Nanak was the founder of the Sikh religion. Many of his early followers were Hindus or Muslims before becoming Sikhs. This story is told about his death.

When Guru Nanak was dying, his followers quarrelled about what should happen to his body when he died. It was the Hindu custom to cremate people. But the Muslims wanted to bury him. They asked Guru Nanak for his decision.

"When I die, cover my body with a shawl," he said. "Then let the Hindus place flowers on one side, the Muslims on the other. The side on which the flowers are still fresh in the morning can choose what to do."

That night, Guru Nanak died and his followers did what he said. In the morning, all the flowers were still fresh. But the Guru's body had gone. The Guru had taught them all an important lesson, that the soul was far more important than the body.

The Golden Temple in Amritsar is the Sikhs' most sacred site.

A day to remember

Every year, in June, Sikhs remember the death of the fifth Guru, Guru Arjan. He built the beautiful Golden Temple in Amritsar, India. In 1606, he was killed by the Mughal (Muslim) emperor of India because of his beliefs. His death is remembered with a full reading of the *Guru Granth Sahib* and a great procession through the streets.

15

A Jewish Funeral

Jewish people believe that you have only one life and death on Earth. They think that you should concentrate on life now and on always living faithfully. Those who lead good lives on Earth will stay with God forever.

A final prayer

When a Jewish person is dying, he or she tries to say a prayer to show that they accept death as God's will. The prayer also asks God to look after the person's family. Another prayer is said by the mourners at the time of death. This is the Shema, the Jews' most important prayer. It sums up what the Jews believe:

'Hear, O Israel,
The Lord is our God. The Lord is One.
Love the Lord your God with all your heart,
And with all your soul,
And with all your might.'

Traditionally, each mourner tears a piece of their clothing to express their feelings of grief. A candle is lit and someone stays with the body until the funeral.

Prayer shawl

Jewish men are often buried in their prayer shawls. However, the fringes at either end of the shawl are removed. This is because they represent the religious rules that Jews observe on Earth, so they are no longer needed after death.

A simple funeral

A Jewish funeral takes place as soon after death as possible, usually within 24 hours. Many Jews bury their dead because they think it is wrong to destroy what God has made. Other Jews allow cremation. The funeral service is very simple, with a plain coffin and no flowers. This is because Jews believe that everyone, rich or poor, is equal

A Jewish cemetery in Jerusalem. The graves are very plain and simple.

The funeral service is conducted by a rabbi.

when they die and should be treated in the same way.

The service at the cemetery is conducted by a rabbi. Prayers are said and there are readings from the holy books. As the coffin is lowered into the grave, the mourners shovel earth on top of it. On their way home, they pluck a few blades of grass to remind themselves that life goes on, even on such a sad occasion.

A special prayer

The Kaddish is the Jewish prayer for the dead. It is recited at the funeral service, every day for 11 months afterwards, and on the anniversary (Yahrzeit) of the death. The prayer is said standing, facing Jerusalem. It is a prayer of praise, both for the good and the bad things that happen in life.

A time of mourning

After the funeral, the family returns home and eats a simple meal of bread and eggs, called the 'meal of comfort'. Over the next seven days, friends and relatives visit the house to offer their prayers and sympathy. The mourners stay at home as a symbol of their grief. This period of seven days is called Shivah (which means seven).

Remembering the dead

A year after the person's death, another ceremony takes place in the cemetery. A simple headstone has been put up at the grave and covered with a cloth. Prayers are said, the cloth removed and the inscription read out loud.

Each year, Jews remember the person who has died. This anniversary is called Yahrzeit. On this day, the family light a candle which burns for 24 hours. They also recite the Kaddish prayer.

Judgement Day

Jews describe their beliefs about life and death in many different ways. In the Hebrew *Bible,* Jews read about Yom Din, or the Day of Judgement. This is the last day, when God will bring the dead back to life and judge them according to their past deeds. This is how death is described in the Book of Daniel:

'And many that sleep in the dust of the earth shall wake up. Some will enjoy ever-lasting life. Others will suffer eternal disgrace. And the wise shall shine with all the brightness of the sky, and those that turn to righteous-ness shall shine like the stars for ever and ever.'
(Daniel 12:2-3)

Jews believe that their holy books tell them how to live. If they obey God's teachings, they will live good lives.

A Yahrzeit candle is lit every year on the anniversary of a person's death. It may be placed next to a photograph of the person who has died.

The rabbi and his sons

This story shows how the Jews try to accept death as God's will.

There was once a rabbi who had two sons. He loved them very much. One terrible day, both sons died. The rabbi was not at home that day. It was Shabbat and he was in the synagogue, teaching people about their faith.

When he returned home, his wife asked him a question.

"A friend gave me two jewels for safe keeping," she said. "And now he wants them back. What shall I do?"

"You must give them back, of course," the rabbi replied.

Then his wife took him by the hand and led him to the room where their sons lay.

"These are the jewels I must give back," she said, sadly.

Through his tears, the rabbi remembered the words of the holy books. He spoke them out loud.

"The Lord has given and the Lord has taken away. Blessed be the Lord."

A NEW LIFE WITH GOD

Christians believe that death is not the end of everything but the start of a new life with God. They believe that Jesus died but he came back to life to be with God for ever. This is called the Resurrection. It shows his followers that they need not be afraid of death.

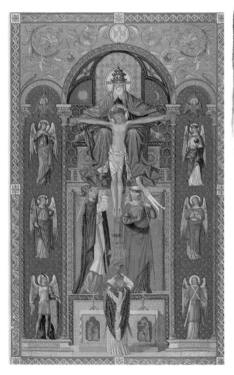

Jesus was put to death on a cross. This is called the Crucifixion. For Christians, the cross is a very important symbol. It reminds them of how Jesus died, and that he came back to life again to give them hope for the future.

Jesus's last days

Every year, at Easter, Christians remember Jesus's death.

At the time of the Passover festival, Jesus went to Jerusalem. He knew his life was in danger. For his teachings had angered the priests and religious leaders. He shared a last meal with his disciples, then went to a nearby garden to pray. While he was there, the temple soldiers came to arrest him. His disciple, Judas, had betrayed him.

The soldiers took Jesus to Pontius Pilate, the Roman governor, who sentenced Jesus to death. That day, he was nailed to a cross made of wood and left to die.

"Forgive them, Lord," Jesus prayed. "For they do not understand their actions."

In the evening, his friends took down his body and placed it in a tomb cut in the rock. They rolled a large stone across the entrance and went sadly away.

It was Friday when Jesus was crucified. His friends thought that they would never see him again. Two days later, on Sunday morning, they went to visit his tomb. To their astonishment, the stone had been

rolled away and the tomb was empty. An Angel, dressed all in white, stood by the tomb and spoke to them.

"Do not be afraid,' the angel said. "I know that you are looking for Jesus who was crucified. He is not here, for he has risen from the dead and is alive."

Jesus's friends were overjoyed. In the following days, Jesus appeared to his friends several times to reassure them and comfort them. Then he climbed the Mount of Olives and was taken to heaven to be with God.

A cemetery in Mexico. Each tomb is built in the shape of a small church.

Wearing black

Christians often wear black at funerals because the dark colour matches the sadness of the occasion. According to folklore, people first wore black for protection. They thought that the dead person's ghost hovered near the body, ready to take a living person for company in the next world. The mourners wore black to avoid standing out in the crowd and attracting the ghost's attention!

Life with God

Christians believe that, through their faith in God, they will share in the Resurrection. Although death is very sad, it is also a time of hope. For Christians, life is like a journey. When they die, they continue on the next stage of their journey and this brings them closer to God. Christians often describe life with God as heaven, and life without God as hell.

A Christian funeral

When a Christian dies, a funeral service is held in a church, chapel or in a crematorium. The coffin is placed before the altar while the priest or minister reads from the *Bible*:

"Jesus said, I am the resurrection and I am the life. If you believe in me, though you may die, yet you will live. Whoever lives and believes in me will never die."
(John 11: 25-6)

The priest also leads prayers to give thanks for the life of the person who has died and to ask God to comfort his or her family and friends. Hymns are sung and there is often a talk about the person's life and work. The service helps to remind Christians of their beliefs and that God's love for them will help to support them in their sadness.

As the priest says the words of the burial service, he throws some earth into the grave. The mourners may also scatter earth or flowers.

Members of the dead person's family help to carry the coffin to the grave.

At the graveside

Some Christians are buried. Others are cremated. While the body is buried or the ashes are scattered, the priest or minister says these words:

"Earth to earth.
Ashes to ashes.
Dust to dust."

This reminds Christians that a person's body is not important. After death, it becomes nothing but ashes, dust or earth. It is their souls which will live on with God.

WATCHED BY ANGELS

When a Muslim dies, the customs and ceremonies followed express Muslim beliefs about life and death. Muslims believe that their lives will be judged by Allah (God) on the Day of Judgement. To make sure that they will be with Allah forever, it is important to lead a good life on Earth. Life is a gift from Allah. It will end when Allah wishes.

Beliefs and prayers

The Prophet Muhammad told his followers that the last words a Muslim should hear are those of the Shahadah, which expresses what Muslims believe:

'There is no God but Allah.
And Muhammad is his messenger.'

There are many other duties to perform when a Muslim dies. The body is taken to the mosque and carefully washed according to Muslim custom. The face, hands and feet are washed first. This is what Muslims do before daily prayers. Then the rest of the body is washed and wrapped in a simple white sheet. All Muslims are treated the same, whether they are rich or poor. The body is then placed in a coffin.

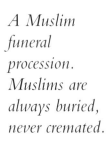

A Muslim funeral procession. Muslims are always buried, never cremated.

Id-ul-Fitr

At the end of Ramadan, the holy month of fasting, Muslims celebrate the festival of Id-ul-Fitr. They exchange cards and gifts with their friends, and have special food to eat. They also visit the graves of relatives who have died, to say prayers.

Two Id (Eid) cards

A Muslim funeral

If possible, the funeral should take place on the day of death. In the mosque, the imam recites the funeral prayer then gives a short talk to the mourners. The imam reminds them of the three most valuable things a good Muslim leaves behind after death.

These are: a good example for children to follow, experience of life which others learn from, and wealth to take care of their family.

Facing Makkah

After this, the coffin is taken to the cemetery. Cremation is forbidden. Muslims are buried facing towards the holy city of Makkah, in Saudi Arabia. At the graveside, the mourners say prayers and recite verses from the *Qur'an*:

"Peace be upon you. May Allah forgive us all. You went to Allah before us and we will follow you." The grave is marked with a simple stone.

An imam leads the funeral prayers.

Angels and judgement

Muslims take comfort from the belief that they will be reunited with their loved ones on the Day of Judgement when Allah will judge them according to how they have lived. They believe that each person has two angels with them throughout their life, keeping a record of their deeds. On the Day of Judgement, the record is handed over to Allah and Allah will judge what each person deserves. Muslims believe that Allah is a fair and merciful judge, ready to forgive people if they are truly sorry for their bad deeds. Good people will be rewarded by drawing closer to Allah in Paradise but wicked people will be punished in Hell. They too may reach Paradise one day through Allah's great mercy.

A Muslim cemetery. The tombs face the holy Muslim city of Makkah in Saudi Arabia.

Mourning customs

The period of mourning usually lasts for 40 days after a death. For the first three days, no cooking is done in the family home. Friends bring food and offer support, comfort and prayers. Sometimes a special meal is held on the seventh and 40th days. There are also prayers to remember the dead person. This is called a rawdah. It is also held on the anniversary of the person's death.

Paradise and Hell

This is how the *Qur'an* vividly describes Paradise and Hell:

'On that day, there will be joyful faces of people in the garden of delights. A gushing fountain shall be there and soft couches with goblets placed before them, silk cushions and rich carpets.'

'On that day, there will be downcast faces of people broken and worn out, burnt by a scorching fire and drinking from a boiling fountain. Their only food will be bitter thorns.'

The Mosque of the Prophet in Madinah is one of the holiest mosques in Islam. It contains the tombs of Muhammad and his close companion, Abu Bakr.

Muhammad's death

In 632 CE, the Prophet Muhammad made a pilgrimage to Makkah from Madinah where he lived. This special journey became known as the Hajj. Every Muslim tries to perform the Hajj at least once in their lifetime. On Mount Arafat, Muhammad preached his last sermon to a crowd of 120,000 pilgrims. He praised and thanked Allah, and told the people to worship Allah and follow his teachings. When he returned to Madinah, Muhammad fell ill and shortly afterwards he died. At first his followers could not believe that he was gone. But Abu Bakr, one of the Prophet's closest companions, reassured them and reminded them that Muhammad had been a messenger of Allah.

Fact Files

Hinduism

- **Numbers of Hindus:** *c.*732 million
- **Where began:** India (*c.* 2500 BCE)
- **Founder figure:** None
- **Major deities:** Thousands of gods and goddesses representing different aspects of Brahman, the great soul. The three most important gods are Brahma the creator, Vishnu the protector, and Shiva the destroyer.
- **Places of worship:** Mandirs (temples), shrines
- **Holy books:** *Vedas*, *Upanishads*, *Ramayana*, *Mahabharata*

Judaism

- **Number of Jews:** *c.* 17 million
- **Where began:** Middle East (*c.* 2000 BCE)
- **Important figures:** Abraham, Isaac, Jacob, Moses
- **Major deities:** One God, the creator who cares for all people.
- **Places of worship:** Synagogues
- **Holy books:** *Tenakh* (Hebrew *Bible*), *Torah* (the first five books of the *Tenakh*), *Talmud*

Buddhism

- **Numbers of Buddhists:** *c.* 314 million
- **Where began:** Nepal/India (6th century BCE)
- **Founder figure:** Siddhartha Gautama, who became known as the Buddha
- **Major deities:** None, the Buddha did not want people to worship him as a god.
- **Places of worship:** Viharas (monasteries or temples), stupas (shrines)
- **Holy books:** *Tripitaka* (*Pali Canon*), *Diamond Sutra* and many others

Christianity

- **Numbers of Christians:** *c.* 2000 million
- **Where began:** Middle East (1st century CE)
- **Important figure:** Jesus Christ
- **Major deities:** One God, in three aspects – as the Father (creator of the world), as the Son (Jesus Christ), and as the Holy Spirit
- **Places of worship:** Churches, cathedrals, chapels
- **Holy books:** *Bible* (Old and New Testaments)

 Sikhism

- **Numbers of Sikhs:** *c.* 18 million
- **Where began:** India (15th century CE)
- **Founder figure:** Guru Nanak
- **Major deities:** One God whose word was brought to people by ten earthly gurus, or teachers.
- **Places of worship:** Gurdwaras (temples)
- **Holy book:** *Guru Granth Sahib*

Islam

- **Numbers of Muslims:** *c.* 1000 million
- **Where began:** Saudi Arabia (*c.* 610 CE)
- **Important figure:** The prophet, Muhammad
- **Major deities:** One God, Allah, who revealed his wishes to the prophet Muhammad.
- **Places of worship:** Mosques
- **Holy books:** The *Qur'an*

GLOSSARY

Allah The Arabic word for God.

Ardas A prayer which is said at the end of all Sikh services.

Brahman The great or supreme soul in Hinduism. Brahman is also called God.

cremation When a dead body is burned to ashes.

crematorium A special building where a body is cremated.

crucifixion Being put to death by being nailed to a cross and left to die, as Jesus was.

dharma An ancient Indian word meaning law or teaching. In Buddhism, it means the Buddha's teaching.

enlightenment Seeing things clearly or as they really are. Realising the truth about life.

gurdwara A Sikh place of worship.

gurmukh 'Filled with God'. Used to describe a very holy Sikh.

Hajj The pilgrimage to Makkah which all Muslims try to make at least once in their lives. This is one of the Five Pillars of Islam.

Id-ul-Fitr A Muslim festival which marks the end of the month of Ramadan.

imam A Muslim who leads the prayers in the mosque.

Kaddish The Jewish prayer for the dead.

karah parshad A sweet food shared out at Sikh services and ceremonies.

karma Your actions and their results, good or bad.

moksha For Hindus, freedom from being born over and over again.

mukti For Sikhs, being set free by God from being born again and again.

nirvana A state of perfect peace and happiness for Buddhists who have gained enlightenment.

Passover A Jewish festival which remembers how Moses led the Jews out of slavery in Egypt. Also called Pesach.

pinda Offerings of rice balls and milk made by Hindus during the period of mourning after a person's death.

rabbi A Jewish religious leader who leads the worship in the synagogue.

Ramadan The Muslim holy month of fasting.

reincarnation Being born again when you die.

Resurrection Jesus's coming back to life after he had been crucified on the cross.

samskara A ceremony which marks a special time in a Hindu's life. There are 16 samskaras in total.

sangha The worldwide family of Buddhists, including monks, nuns and ordinary people.

Shema An important Jewish prayer which reminds Jews to love and worship God.

Shivah The seven days of mourning in a Jewish home. Shivah means 'seven'.

Sohila The Sikh evening prayer or hymn.

stupa A dome-shaped Buddhist shrine. Stupas sometimes contain the ashes of important monks, others contain sacred texts.

Yahrzeit A ceremony held on the anniversary of a Jewish person's death.

Yom Din The Jewish Day of Judgement.

INDEX